AWAY

AWAY

*Poems
by
Andrew Salkey*

Allison & Busby
London and New York

First published 1980 by
Allison and Busby Limited
6a Noel Street, London W1V 3RB, England
and distributed in the USA by
Schocken Books Inc, 200 Madison Avenue, NY 10016

Salkey, Andrew
  Away.
  I. Title
  811 PR9265.9.S2A/ 80-40643

  ISBN 0-85031-337-6
  ISBN 0-85031-338-4 Pbk

  LC- 80-4-643

Set in Garamond by Malvern Typesetting Services
and printed in Great Britain by
Biddles Ltd, Guildford, Surrey

Acknowledgements

Some of the poems in this book were first published in the following political journals, newspapers, literary magazines and anthologies, whose editors we thank for permission to reprint the poet's work here: *Caliban* (USA); *Contrast* (Canada); *Corlit* (Trinidad); *Kontakto Antiyano* (Holland); *Little Word Machine* (UK); *New Letters* (USA); *New Poetry 1* and *New Poetry 2: Arts Council Anthologies* (UK); *Okike* (USA); *Outlet* (Antigua); *Ploughshares* (USA); *Poetry Information* (UK); *Race Today* (UK); *Sechaba* (UK); *Tapia* (Trinidad); *Third World Newsletter* (USA); *Trinidad Guardian* (Trinidad); and *Workshop New Poetry* (UK).

Bring me the sunflower for me to transplant
to my own ground burnt by the spray of sea . . .

Eugenio Montale   from ''Bring me the sunflower'', in *Selected*
                   Poems of Eugenio Montale (Penguin Modern
                   European Poets, 1969)

Contents

PART ONE

Away

Your boat is going, I see;
take me, friend, in your boat,
I'm going to the sea.

Nicolás Guillén   from ''I'm going to Wuhan'',
taken from *Tengo*

Away

(FOR CHARLES HYATT)

I hold a banyan of memories of home
in my head; I have a Rio Bueno of slides:
an unbroken flow of air mail envelopes,
their zig-zag borders carrying on and on,
until the unseen sender returned and died;
someone else, just as faithful, a Harriet
who stayed beside me but who also died;
a large dining-room blackboard on which
singular verb matched singular subject;
that end-and-beginning-of-year Swift ham,
brown with sugar and jabbed black with cloves;
the slow, slow understanding of '38;
those very painful examination years;
the inconsolable lack of a community bell;
abeng, broken again and again, and discarded;
the lizard on its back; the waste of men;
the long line of women at the bottom of the hill;
the warmth that goes for nothing; the lies;
the story no leader will tell; the drift;
the blaze of poinsettias; the sunset at sunrise;
the burning image of West Kingston as hell.

The voices in my room say something, perhaps
nothing at all that really means anything.
And yet, they persist. They claim they have a way
with history, with all the people who make it.
Meanwhile, the everlasting banyan spiders the earth
and slowly penetrating Rio Bueno flows and flows.

Sweet Mango

Away, here I am,
in search of a country,
trying hard to find myself
a land of fruit trees
to return to,
a sweet mango, perhaps,
with my mother's face
on its slowly yellowing skin,
my father's own exile
scattered among the leaves,
my brother's immaturity
and my own
nervously leaping
up and down
on the stones and trash
which hide the roots
from all of us.

Two

Once a firm-voiced, hard-nerved house
surrounded her early-morning movements;
children, like rushing corpuscles,
defended her sea-split marriage
which she supported like a harvest tray
right up to the end of the return journey.

We all fight back on a shoe-string,
she might have said had you touched her
where the torture-marks still burn;
but she lived two broken lives as one,
and chose silence as her way of coping.

After a Long Time Away

That necessary visit,
that regretted return,
that very first
and, so far, last look back,
that very late overview!

How the broken gate,
smashed fence,
cracked stones;
how the scooped-out red earth,
small, open rooms,
men like boys;
how the slack jaw-line,
diminished authority
and obvious loopholes
hit the visiting eye!'

A violent neighbour,
an outside uncle, some say,
with large, veined arms akimbo,
feet apart, his all-round household,
area whip-hand all too apparent,
throws hard, green mangoes
at the rooting dogs
in their own back yard!

Of course,
we all come to know,
sooner or later,
that quick, sinking feeling

of shock we get
when we find the house
we once lived in
(slowly grew tall in,
became suddenly wise
out of the experiences
we enticed in, again and again,
like a tightly-stoked
pitch-pine fire),
now, somehow, looking
smaller and shabbier
than we remembered it,
in our Atlantic-divided mind,
throughout the years
we spent running away from it.

Gone Away

Rage
at her extended family's
self-contempt
rose up
in her throat
like the island's history
as she washed her hands
in the thin column
of taxed water
in the disused kerosene can.

All her slave ships,
that day,
were splintered masts,
whittled sticks,
murderous knives,
poised for the plunge,
held low above her head,
just above her attempts
at flight.

When she cried out
(an assertion that startled
the cluttered harbour yard),
her words sprang
like switch-blades,
finding the heart of the matter,
centuries of *becoming*
quickly turning to *being*,
at last.

Turning Slowly Away

A row of eucalyptus trees,
a fence of bamboo shoots,
a hedge of joseph's-coat:
home on the retina;

his eyes, turning slowly,
turning, turning slowly away:
a creaking electric fan,
a Sunday procession;

daily doubts, coming and going:
a slow pendulum rope,
a jalousie banging in the wind,
a surprise spray of maidenhair fern;

he looked inside the room
but recollection had already broken into it;
he looked into the mirror:
a record as empty as a crater;

he had deliberately lost himself:
an exile of expectation,
an exile of chance hope,
an exile preparing to move on.

Land Fly 'Way

Well, now,
Tata was a man
who like to fuck,
and that make Tata
a most ordinary
world sort o' man
on the land.

But, what happen
to poor Tata luck
is that him woman
fly 'way to America,
figuring say that that
is where Tata strength
actual gone to.

We Left Home, Because

Based on a conversation with a St
Lucian worker in Birmingham

We tried
to reach you,
with love,
from the hurt
where we stood,
in the hole.

We tried
to feed ourselves,
with our hands,
from the land
we thought
was our own.

We tried
to live,
at home,
where we imagined
we really
belonged.

We left,
only when we knew
we weren't
part of the plan
and weren't meant
to be.

[19]

Delroy Smallpiece Away from St Thomas

He left home
and walked into a world
of multi-plant undertakings,
dispute- and grievance-procedures
and disciplinary matters;

he stepped off
his first red bus,
down on to several column inches
on the financial page
of a newspaper
which had a lot to say
about the application
of the Code of Industrial Relations Practice
in small establishments;

the paper flapped a little
in the swirl of a fake wind
near St Giles Circus,
and he glimpsed an exhortation
about building societies
and a headline
about the commercial activities
of certain professional footballers;

that night, television told him
about the Anglo-Saxon vagaries
of retail distribution,
consumer protection,

the clothing trades,
paper-box manufacturing,
and about the shaky state
of industrial relations
in six unnamed British firms;

later,
hopelessly snarled
in a conflict between London
and night jasmine, rural sounds
and stand-pipe chatter,
he slept uneasily
in his ill-chosen country of shopkeepers.

Strong, Silent Man

(FOR JOHN HOWIE)

At the end
of the maritime day,
stillness
is all we've got,
like a parking lot
vacated
by the confident drivers
downtown.

Later on,
ocean shadows
bring
night's eternity,
and the uncertainty
and silence
that drag us
back to truth.

Writing Away from Home

"Literature is made of remembrance."
Isaac Bashevis Singer

All the green leaves
seem to be turning brown
in her clenched fist
of lost chances;

when she looks
along the veins of her arms,
she sees that either
the old roads have disappeared

or the land
and its rich surprises
have been renamed with new hopes
and newer policy aspirations;

she and most of us, outside,
live half in doubt,
half by intuition,
feeling our way with memory.

Drifting

For whom do I speak, now,
so far away from home?
For whom do I write, now,
so far away from myself?

I speak for the experience
of the flux I've become;
I write for the concrete
to fill in the distances

from the house on the road
I lived on, from the warm
home on the sea I crossed,
from old voices to the new.

And I suppose that's true,
to some extent, of shipping
oneself far away from port,
finding oneself while drifting.

Annotated Latin Text at Stanford

(FOR GREGSON DAVIS AND MARGO DAVIS)

Slicing your way through the elegant treacheries
of the dead language, opening it all out
for the benefit of your students, that morning,
hoping (as we know you do) to reveal
a living literature, buried deep
in figures of speech and cold ashes
with meaning and truths still capable
of touching the mist of shaky California,
given the chance, somewhere along the fault,

we left you alone, for San Francisco,
a home from home for so very many,
earthquake ribbons in her hair,
a sweet, pulsing Babel on her lips.

Let's chat about language, too ancient
for some, too demotically new for others!
Let's chat about it, classical or modern,
when we make it build myths for our protection,
when we make it sing lies for our escape!

Later, we loved it patiently with a camera:
shot after shot of a three-day visitor,
seeing home for the first time in America,
intending to surprise himself by saying yes,
and yet knowing that he, too, would be left
slicing his way through the sparkling treacheries
of the new land, committedly and alone, sooner
or later, Pacific lights in his eyes.

Landscape after Retirement

(FOR ST CLAIR DRAKE)

Chicago: like the back of your hand;
the earlier railroad, the same..

Just as heavily veined and stressed,
you know and carry with you whole

all our suffering: a spread of pain
which, we know, you conceal quietly.

After reading "There Is A Tree More Ancient Than Eden"

(FOR LEON FORREST)

I like your way of seeing the flux and rush
of everything as a sure way of seeing clearly
everything there is to see; I really do.

As a flood-man myself, born just below
your house, and in a house like yours,
I'm sure you know I understand your way.

It's mine, too. But my thing's been rushed
off centre by living years away from home,
by seeing everything in bits and pieces,

not as the whole you know you see yours as,
flooding along the freeway (in name only),
making it all seem logically yours and bearable.

Yet, I do know your way; I think I know it well,
like the inevitable downpour from the hills,
the *yes* and *no* of everything we live through.

I like your way of seeing it; I like it just as though
I'd dredged it up myself and made it all my own,
living, as I do, absurdly far away from home.

Notting Hill Carnival, 1975

Souse, fried fish and mauby,
magical pan, band and float,
costume, swagger and jump-up:
Carnival can't leap the Gulf!

Pick up the Port of Spain display,
complete in the head of the *mas*,
throw it straight across the water
and watch it drop flat and splayed
like a two-day anniversary drunk,
tricked and freaked out as we are,
stepping high, all over the Grove!

Look at the frantic stamp-and-go,
the tugging muddle in the mind,
the heavy hesitation over play,
the forced glinting tone-and-flash,
the tepid menace of the masquerade,
as losers trip and fake bacchanal,
stumbling, up and down the Grove!

Forget the slide of immigration;
simply mime the dreams of exile;
dress the naked pain with images
of history texts, sea and planets
and cross the road with metaphor,
knowing how short ten years are
to squeeze home, into the Grove!

Souse, fried fish and mauby,
magical pan, band and float,
costume, swagger and jump up:
Carnival can't leap the Gulf!

History and Away

(FOR ELSA GOVEIA)

What we do with time
and what time does with us
is the way of history,
spun down around our feet.

So we say, today,
that we meet our Caribbean shadow
just as it follows the sun,
away into the curve of tomorrow.

In fact, our sickle of islands
and continental strips are mainlands
of time with our own marks on them,
yesterday, today and tomorrow.

Garvey, Padmore, Fanon: Why Didn't They Return?

(IN MEMORY OF MY MOTHER)

The man in white returned.
But look back, now, at how
he ended up high on the hog,
leaving the dirty water dirtier,
leaving the narrow streets,
climbing the foothills!

Leaving,
always leaving
once they return,
they return only
to leave us, again!

Why didn't *they* return?

Why did *he* bother?
Was it only to stir up the gutter wash,
renew his exile,
use poverty shrewdly,
snatch property,
get in, get out, again,
leaving everything the same?

Leaving,
always leaving
once they return,
they return only
to leave us, again!

Why didn't *they* return?

Why didn't *they* return,
Africa on their minds,
our Caribbean in gully dust,
Africa, vast enough
to dream about working for,
old enough to escape to,
deep enough to drown in,
home, far enough away from home?

Leaving,
always leaving
once they return,
they return only
to leave us, again!

Why didn't *they* return?

Remember Haiti, Cuba, Vietnam

Here's something folk tales tell
us about, at night, but which
we lose sight of during the day:

Giants can be surprised.

That's something three slingshots
in our third of the world gauged
and defiantly stretched to success.

What's the light like now in the dark?

Look at the untouched stones
lying on our beaches
and the idle rubber bands
in our upturned hands!

In the Indian Nation

(FOR ROBERT TISDALE AND DAGMAR TISDALE)

No reservation-marks stabbed the earth
round her house of stitched dreams;
yes, the ones the new families spaced out
were there, all right, after they swelled
with land-grab and possession-fevers,
hers dying, as the sunflowers cracked the sky.

She sits, now, pricking her fingertips
with borrowed needle and thread,
all her land and water spread out round her,
her proud old family-names spacing out
the murderous theft and scorpion-treaties,
small town dust feathering her hands and tired eyes.

Home Parables

1. FRINGE BENEFITS

Through the rip in her gingham dress,
a slash of thigh streaked
high across the retina.

Lonely as a mouse, she'd come to town
to work as a servant girl,
in that house, in Stony Hill.

At the back, her shrunken room,
a convenient, early morning lay-by
for the drunken paymaster!

She'd said nothing about her three children
who stayed at home in Saint Elizabeth,
because she wasn't paid to talk.

Late that Saturday night, the paymaster
brought his five non-paying friends to her room,
but she refused without saying a word.

Later that drunken Sunday morning,
the paymaster sent her back to the country,
without his wife suspecting a thing.

But the fated girl from Saint Elizabeth
had the last laugh, as she pensively pressed
the bulging pockets of her gingham dress,

thought about her three children
and deliberated on the crisp reparations,
snug in the six wallets she'd just liberated.

2. STOCK-TAKING

She was a barmaid and a half,
caring profoundly for bottle and drinker
with a fierce Kingston pride.

Loss was today's gain of tourists;
profit, tomorrow's small change regulars,
their unbankable dreams and all.

Naturally, the bar wasn't hers,
but she managed like a burr
on a snapped shoe-string.

And then came that sudden strike
and the mouths to ply with credit
and the dreams she had to support.

In the end, the stock ran dry;
the owner refused to believe;
some of the regulars lost heart.

But she found a way round it,
by believing in the strike
and subsidising it on the sly.

Bottles appeared on the shelves
from cool and unrevealed sources;
the owner turned a blind eye.

But what the louse hadn't seen was just
how far the ownership of the bar had changed;
it was now a repossessed *public* house.

3. FUTURISTIC HISTORY TEACHER

She'll say historically piquant,
conspiratorial things like, "Columbus,
that Genoese, was really a Jew, you know!

"He kept on fooling Ferdinand and Isabella
with promises of gold, but was actually looking
for a new home for the Jews, this side of the world."

Then, she'll sigh an under-celebrated Clio sigh,
and go on to add, "Why, of course, I must tell you
that the Caribbean was never intended for us!

"In fact, we wouldn't have been brought over here
at all, had Columbus's clandestine,
clannish plan worked out all right.

"But he believed his own story of gold so much
that it popped up to the surface
of everything he touched, coldly taking him over.

"There's absolutely no doubt whatsoever that both
Spain and the Jews were tricked; but so were we
by that Euro-Arab commercial get-together."

Then, she'll hold the approved history text,
pretty far away from her formidable breasts,
and ask, "What's this, anyway?"

We'll know her own reply so well
that we'll raise the tops of our desks,
and yell, "Yet another slick conspiracy!"

PART TWO

I never left

I am like a tree in flower
that yesterday was neither.

Nicolás Guillén   from "I am like a tree in flower",
taken from *Tengo*

a novel left

I Never Left

Written after many readings of Anna Akhmatova's
"I am not one of those who left the land . . ."

Yes, I am one of those
who left the island;
but I am also one of those few
who remained behind;
I never left.

I stood up to the glasshouses,
sugar refracted in their prisms;
Caribbea's labour looked structured,
polished and monumental;
I faced shadows in limping London
and, for short bursts,
in demented New York
and mean-spirited Paris,
where they all see
splintered reflections of their past,
over there, anywhere,
already proving a shared alienation
too visibly, too palpably, here,
but where I respond all of a piece
as my old, new self, spliced,
locked and bolted by the sea
I never left.

The songs I hummed away from home,
then and now, were not
and can't be folk songs
earning metropolitan slaps on the back;
they've always been authentic;
they've always sounded distant,
out of true, out of the place
I never left.

Just consider, for a moment, the style
of some of those who stayed.
Dry land tourists! Inner émigrés!
North Americans deferred!
Incredible mirror images!
Shouldn't they have gone abroad,
instead of staying put
and being so far removed
from the native truth?
Instead of turning away
from the guinep tree,
the restlessness of the sea;
instead of exiling myself
away from my everydayness,
I left the island
so that I wouldn't have to leave;
I left the island
I never left.

Looking Back

(FOR JESSICA HUNTLEY)

I can't understand why we beat the sea
with our island pain and aspiration;
I can't understand why we deny ourselves
our sea-locked gold reserves, stacked
high in the hills, plaited deep in the land.

The truth is: I'm beginning to know why
all the eyes in our mirror are turned north
and north-east. Isn't it really because
we haven't looked at the arc of our lives
in the cloud and curve of our breathprints?

A Memory of Jasmine

(FOR JANET COLLINS)

Seeing you so clearly,
so far away from home
(myself an aging exile),
I realised a delicacy
of jasmine had taken root
inside an alien door.

And don't they say that
far-away perfumes open
all padlocked houses,
even the winter ones,
somebody èlse's, as love
and night jasmine do?

Long Years Away from Home

J, a fabric designer, remembers how to make a
simple, strong tie-dye for her studio needs

(FOR TREVOR MUNROE)

She told us she had forgotten
that the crushed pebble seeds
of the ordinary annotto tree,
mixed with some ordinary rum,
would certainly give her back
a bowl of remarkable red dye.

Postcard from Martinique, 25.vii.1972

(FOR SUZANNE PINTARD)

Thanks for small favours
done for her, casually,
in hutched London,
and a lighthearted tone
of Caribbean promise,
written in a post office,
in Fort de France,
in an island nowhere near
its people's own!

The stamp,
a little, revenue-grabbing
fifty-centime
cherry-pink Frankish head,
boasts *République Française*;

the picture on the front,
captioned on the left top back
Costumes créoles
(*Groupe folklorique martiniquais*),
a calculated tourism winner;

six Black women
(on whom *rayonnement* has long shone),
dressed in bandanas, aprons,
full ankle-length skirts
and strings of beads
(all shrewdly borrowed,
for the duration of the pose,
from *la belle époque*
and continuing colonial pain),
have left the lush fruit trees
and clustered blossoms behind,
and are now safely back,
far west of *la douce France*,
back in yesterday's stranglehold.

Postcard from Mexico, 16.x.1973

(FOR ANNE WALMSLEY)

From Villahermosa,
in Tabasco,
out of the lowlands
of Veracruz
(Chiapas
only spitting distance away),
an upright, giant
Olmec head,
without benefit of clergy,
brings moonfaced greetings
on its African lips,
three thousand years old;

and the liana-twined palimpsest
of myth and mysterious history,
flat on the table before me,
says its message is clear,
says it swallowed whole
the Mexican Revolution,
says its head grew larger and larger
with headache after headache
at watching the progress
of Mexico's bouncing economy
leaping north over the border
like jumping beans nobody sees.

Look,
no Mexicans!

[46]

Postcard from Brazil, 8.i.1974

(FOR NOEMIA GUERRA)

The sentiments of the painter,
visiting voluntary exile,
were appropriately wishful:
"I am in Bahia.

"It is wonderful
to see again
the landscape
we love.

"I am 'recharging my battery'
for the next period of work."

Yes, maybe,
in a country
that plays *Jõgo de Capoeira*
on a *cartão postal*
with the irony
of a *Rua Chile* postmark;

but, surely,
not anywhere near
thrusting, supercharged,
nightmare Brazil,
where murder
is the name of the game?

Postcard from Uganda, 14.i.1974

(FOR MARINA OMOWALE MAXWELL)

Wild Life from East Africa,
Elephant:
legend;

Kampala, Uganda:
smudged postmark;

"Enjoying every minute,
and somehow
I'm going to live in Africa
for a good long stretch."
Your traveller's words,
hopeful as *poui*;

but, then, you ended
by saying: "Hope to see you,
if I get to U.K."

Now, by Kampala standards,
anything (gesture, word
or document) with an "if"
could look like, sound like,
and, in fact, be like
doubt, or much, much more.

New élites nurture
imagined slights:
another legend
or presidential *hubris*;

stampedes of good intentions,
during short trips to Mother,
just simply can't compare
with the elephantiasis
of lurking lorries and tanks;

and, of course, it's said
they've got brakes, all right,
but also accurately turreted guns
which the pathfinding drivers use
like trickily angled headlights
to find their vanguard way home.

Postcard from Jamaica, 19.iv.1974

(FOR AUBREY WILLIAMS)

Pictures of home, even those published
and sold with hustling pride by a gem

like The Novelty Trading Company Limited
(a name as near a commercial euphemism
as any Madison Avenue copywriter can get
for our kind of quick-sell independence
and brand-new, advertised nationhood),

and looked at, from any convenient angle,
in my sun-deprived Bayswater rooms,

mongoose these Turner-conditioned eyes
with broad daylight spinels of new colours,
once unnoticeably native to me as breathing;

your easy-going affectionately chosen
Overlooking Ocho Rios from Shaw Park Gardens
levered my own recall of those resonant
landscape figures, not intended to be apparent

in the rich greenery and deep Carib blue water,
trapped in your discriminating picture postcard:

those paunchy remittance lounge-lizards,
Southern cracker-brown beachcombers,
sneakingly lecherous spiritual advisers;

those fruit-, fish-, eggs-, vegetables-,
steak-importing, island-insulting hoteliers,
those tax-exempted, profits-exporting,
unseen Northern investment-saviours;

those sinful answers to Tourist Board prayers
in that happy Schnorkel paradise of ours!

I've read and re-read your brotherly note,
and it tells me, time and time again,
everything I already know, my own exile's story,
but in your unique visitor's narrative:

"Me bwoy,
Things have been impossible
but very good.

"Leaving for Miami,
now."

And that nice nomad's afterthought:
"Will contact you, again,
from there."

Soufrière

(FOR ROBERT AND MADDIE MÁRQUEZ)

Far and wide
outside St Vincent,
the man, who holds
the Soufrière postcard,
regrets the energy
used so prettily,
stilled by a stamp,
approved with a postmark,
tamed by firm fingers.

At this time, in America,
they'd tell you, Soufrière,
"Keep on keepin' on!"

For you've been a long time
on the boil, bulked
and gorged with layers
of hot rock and soup thick
earth, rolled in folds,
pleated and tucked
into molten waves
of mounting resentment
and anger, banging inside
the field-slave's head
for luck: see how he squints
like clinking marbles;
listen to him gritting his ancient teeth!

Bite, Soufrière, bite through
that top lip of ours,
through our bauxite gardens,
bordered by sugar cane and bananas!

How many of us know
how to wait for the gush
to blow, for the ashes
to cool, for the rocks
to dry, for the stone
to be handed on, deep
inside St Vincent and far
and wide outside?

Dry River Bed

"He (the returned migrant worker) has changed faster than his country. The economic conditions which form his decision to leave have not improved; they may have deteriorated."

John Berger and Jean Mohr, from *A Seventh Man*

Poem inspired by my reading of "Part 3: Return" of the Text

he came back
by 'plane,
train,
bus
and cart

his expectations
were plain:
family,
eyecorner familiarity,
back-home self,
or so he thought

1.
during the last stretch,
on foot,
over the hard dirt road,
a beggar smiled at him,
and held out his left hand,
like a reaping hook

he gave him
nearly all his small change

2.
further along the way,
a tatter of children
offered him pebbly mangoes,
at a price

he handed over
the rest of his change,
without taking the mangoes

3.
on the narrative veranda,
where all the village tales
had perched
and taken off again,
his mother stood,
as light as the money
he'd just given away

in his embrace,
her body, wrapped wire,
felt smaller
than he remembered,
her face drawn tight
and frightened

4.
everything was diminished,
whittled by long urban knives:
the road outside,
the front garden,
the lean-to house,
the back yard,
the lives

5.
all his family
and neighbours
were knocking softly
at death's door,
waiting patiently,

spit fringing their cracked lips,
wizened frowns
sliding
into their collapsed cheeks

6.
the villagers clawed at him
and what little he'd brought back;

they picked him clean
as a eucalyptus

7.
he quickly saw
that home was a dry river bed;
he knew he'd have to run away, again,

or stay and be clawed to death
by the eagle
hovering over the village;
nothing had changed

8.
he walked alone,
for a while;
not even his footprints
sank behind him,
in the dust;

no niche,
no bounce-back,
no mirror, anywhere,
in which to see himself,
merely the sunlight
mocking everybody, everywhere,
and the circling eagle

Georgetown Gal

(FOR ENID HOUSTY)

Georgetown Gal,
Guyana cawn know
the magic them got
in dat sweet head o yours!

Is blind them blind
or wha?

You mustn mind them,
you hear!

Is the people them
we want
an the people ways
we want
an is them dreams them
we want
an the diamonds
lightin up you head.

Is that all o we
lovin you for,
same so,
Georgetown Gal!

PART THREE

Only change will do

de people demma fite
fe stay alive dung deh
de people demma fite
fe dem rites dung deh

de people demma fite
oppreshan dung deh
de people demma fite
fe dem life dung deh

Linton Kwesi Johnson from ''Com wi goh dung deh'',
taken from *Dread Beat and Blood*

Only Change Will Do

The love of the home I left
is the art of the impossible;
to keep loving it is easier
than going straight back to it.

The Oppression of the Gift

For hulking Kingston swaggerers
they walked politically prettily,

balancing empty policy
with emptier promises
and cheap personal hand-outs,

when they made their short rum
and water visits, out of town.

That was and still is their way
of keeping the oppression of the gift

going, of further holding open
the upturned calloused hands,
and closing the future,

under a binding sweaty obligation,
sealed with a slap on the back and a wink.

Tropical Beauty

This picture-postcard language,
flat as tinted photographic truth,
was processed to paint lies,
to drag back in
the privileged flies,
to make a fool
of the wise fisherman.

And, of course,
we all know
that the place is beautiful,
with logwood blossoms,
mimosa
and falls
and lily-white sand,
and that most of the people
are not picturesquely poor!

But is that enough?
Is that really enough?

Lion Tamers

(FOR THE REVOLUTIONARY WOMEN FIGHTERS IN THE ERITREAN
LIBERATION MOVEMENT)

"All the world is underdeveloped and the proof is
the existence of the Third World."
Josué de Castro

I'm looking at a group picture of you,
published in a safe Sunday newspaper,
spread wide on a family table,
thousands of tightwire miles away
from your lion-hunting silence.

Your faces are all set against
the world's hill and gully
and your own flat savannah,
reported only during every other drought,
every other famine, every other genocide,
across the centuries of leonine serfdom,
across the uselessness of the burnt grass,
across the stench of the stinging wind.

You sit down now with your re-educated men,
the unity healing the ancient divisions
with touching elbows and shoulders,
locking out the crippling solitude
with matching dreams and actions.

At this distance, even I can hear
the dying swish of the useless tail,
the hereditary roar dropped to a moan,
the old lion house crumbling away,
the new land rising slowly in your eyes.

[64]

Palm-Kernel Cutter

The palm kernel
is all his world;

it carries him
from harvest
to poverty;

he carries it
stuck on the point
of his upturned cutlass
like a severed Gambian head
from the city
which means
he's capable
of dropping it
any time he wants to.

After they Brush the Crumbs Away

(FOR JOHN KANI AND WINSTON NTSHONA)

"Just as people do not love alike, neither do they starve alike."

From a review (by Ronald Blythe in *The Listener*, 28. ii. 1974)
of Knut Hamsun's *Hunger*, translated by Robert Bly,
introduced by Robert Bly and Isaac Bashevis Singer.

Those whom we left behind
when we took history's trail abroad;
those whom we left sitting
on the hillside slope
with their backs resting
on the brightly-painted, substantial
up-for-sale signs,
on the bank by the dry river-bed,
by the dusty roadway to the airport;
they all seem unable to die of hunger,
like the screen and magazine millions
in the Emperor's barracoons,
Mahatma's vast back yard,
Mohammed's mountain wastelands,
Soweto's steam-heat dirt-track,
Bolivia's brutal other world
and everywhere else on the wrong side
of the long line of fat;
they all seem unable to die like flies
some paid writers, isolated sweetly,
in paradise and recognition,
theoretically complain.

[66]

It's possible, at a guess, I suppose,
that those story-tellers see the sun
making a crucial difference
to the spreading fainting-spell,
axing pain in the head,
spit-fringed lips,
drooping shoulders,
skin tight rib-cage,
premature grey hair,
closed ministry doors,
bureaucratic hush,
absence of welfare,
like an aching amputation.

Those who starve,
starve and starve alike;
we who look on,
reading or writing
in a cool room
or in a deeply-heated one,
look alike;
the sun shines down
on both clusters of the dying,
at home
and abroad.

Rays of Hope

(FOR JUDY RAY AND DAVID RAY)

"Back in 1968, when (the South Africans) were explaining why blacks were not in their national swimming teams, the then-president of the SA National Olympics Council told a magazine: 'The Africans show no interest in swimming, because the water clogs their pores and they tire easily.'

. . . During his recent trip to the Republic, former junior Australian surfing champion, Peter Drouyn, just happened to pick up the idea that 'the coloured people there are afraid of the water.' He told *The Australian*, in Sydney: 'They consider the surf a voodoo area, and, as a consequence, they don't develop surfing talent.'"

The Guardian, 8. i. 1975

You should've seen
who struggled out of the sea,
today: a tired, rock-sliced
miner, with clogged pores,
who'd given up the race,
foxing them completely,
locking his hands
into the sand!

You should've seen him:
wrong apparatus
for the daily splash,
wrong everything
for the long-distance swim,
but with eyes that see
Voortrekkers'-end
in the kidney-shaped
competitive water
across the happy
holiday posters!

[68]

But you should've seen
the others! They were chalky
with stolen mineral dust,
and for ever heading
to the sea, Boer ghosts,
scrambling, land-crazed
diamond-swipers,
strong swimmers to a *baas*,
who know deep down
(as non-swimming
Luthuli told us)
that they've got to hit
that southern water,
some segregated day soon,
remarkable pores and all,
orchids in their hair,
and with their nasal Dutch Christ
cheering them along,
all the way out,
to the wide, quiet Antarctic.

A Born Fighter

(FOR RICARDO MACEO MÁRQUEZ)
b. Friday, 7 March 1975

You come
of fighters

and you came fighting
into the world

in a month
named after a warrior

one of your own names
the name of a *Comandante* we love

But you also come
of love

and you came loved
into the world

in a house
of hope

strong with life lines
fused as one love

Deep Footprints

On Ho Chi Minh's birthday
19 May 1975

Once, we had a persistent uncle,
with us, at home, a slow burner,
with more than enough patience
to light the whole family fire.

We called him names like hope,
work, struggle, time and victory;
his smile hid years of torment;
his walk was slow and very long.

When he died, the whole family
called one another names like hope,
work, struggle, time and victory;
and his footprints became ours.

"We must become hard, but we must never lose tenderness"

Che

(FOR ZOË BEST)

Facing up to ourselves,
looking into the glare
of the pouncing mirror,
during the slow march
of lies, steeped in aid,
spread very far and wide
with long liana strings
that tie our feet quietly,
confuse and turn us round,
we should become the bole
of an old Guyanese *mora*,
standing as far inside
as possible from the cold
continental shore, pressing
for ever forward from behind
a campaign-push for years
at a time; we should become
more like the valid ground
we stand on, hard with history.

Yet, we must cup our hands
for water from the creek;
we must live plaited lives,
woven bamboo strips, touching
one another, always holding
the trembling hand, at night,
taking the strain, bridging
cut faiths, for ever caring,
while knowing everything
that White Antelope knew,
knowing that, in fact,
"Nothing lives long; only
the earth and the mountains."

El Mio Mar

(FOR NICOLÁS GUILLÉN)

I believe
the reason
for your undersea power,
deep, as it is,
around our submerged mountain peaks,
is so that you'll protect
the breathless runner on the sand;
there's no other reason
for your forests of ozone
surrounding our islands.

Waterpower cartwheels through
the spokes of the starfish!

El mio mar,
you're usually ignored,
except on photogenic moonlight nights,
when you float cargo bits in your hair,
carpenters'-twists for curls,
or when some penetration or other
is northernly necessary for capital
and containment; but I know
your waves promise to bunch and blow away
the old cash-and-carry, some hurricane soon.

Moonlight lattices through
the mangrove swamps!

I believe,
Caribbea,
that our recurring Sargasso dream
is surely one in which
your swirling bob-and-weave
is naturally ours to bank on;
there's no other reasonable way
of looking at you,
either close up, at home,
or from this cold distance, with love.

Sargasso strangles everything
but the green glimmer of plankton!

Summer Song

There seems almost nothing
to hold on to, now; nothing;

home drifts on farther away
like a late wish in the wind;

and the corner I stand in
seems frozen over and dead.

*"There's nothing, here, now;
nothing, back there, either!"*

Whispers sneak over everything;
everything's cold and clear.